BIRDS FROM MY WINDOW

A Collection of Australian Bird Haiku and Art

M Perumal

All rights reserved.

No part of this publication may be reproduced, distributed, or transmitted by any person or entity in any form or by any means, including photocopying (except under the statutory provisions of the Australian *Copyright Act 1968*), recording, or other electronic or mechanical methods, without the prior written permission of the author. Any unauthorised distribution or use of this text/artwork may be a direct infringement of the author's rights and those responsible may be liable in law accordingly.

Copyright © M Perumal 2024

The moral right of the author has been asserted.

Book Cover by M Perumal

Illustrations by M Perumal

1st edition published by Leaf & Line Designs in 2024

For my family,

who give me a million reasons
to smile every day.

Author's note

Let me begin with a huge thank you to you for picking up this little book of haiku and art. This book has been a labour of love - for the nature that surrounds me, for writing, for art, and for a tiny little dream I had of having a book out there with my name on it.

I am neither a bestselling poet nor am I an accomplished artist. This little book is not going to change the world. Yet I like what I do, and by putting this book out there, I am hoping that my words and art will resonate with some of you.

This book was inspired the the birds I saw from my window - literally. Living by the mountains in Melbourne, Australia brings me much entertainment in the guise of cheeky cockatoos, colourful lorikeets, scheming magpies and the iconic kooraburra. I've heard birds that I cannot identify, and the odd mynah makes an appearance every now and then.

I hope you enjoy this journey through my world as much as I've enjoyed sharing it with you.

M Perumal

Table of contents

Cover
Title Page
Copyright
Author's Note
Artwork 1 (spread)
Haiku 1
Haiku 2
Haiku 3
Artwork 2
Haiku 4
Haiku 5
Artwork 3
Haiku 6
Artwork 4 (spread)
Haiku 7
Haiku 8
Haiku 9
Artwork 5
Haiku 10
Haiku 11
Artwork 6
Haiku 12
Haiku 13
Artwork 7
Haiku 14
Haiku 15
Artwork 8 (spread)

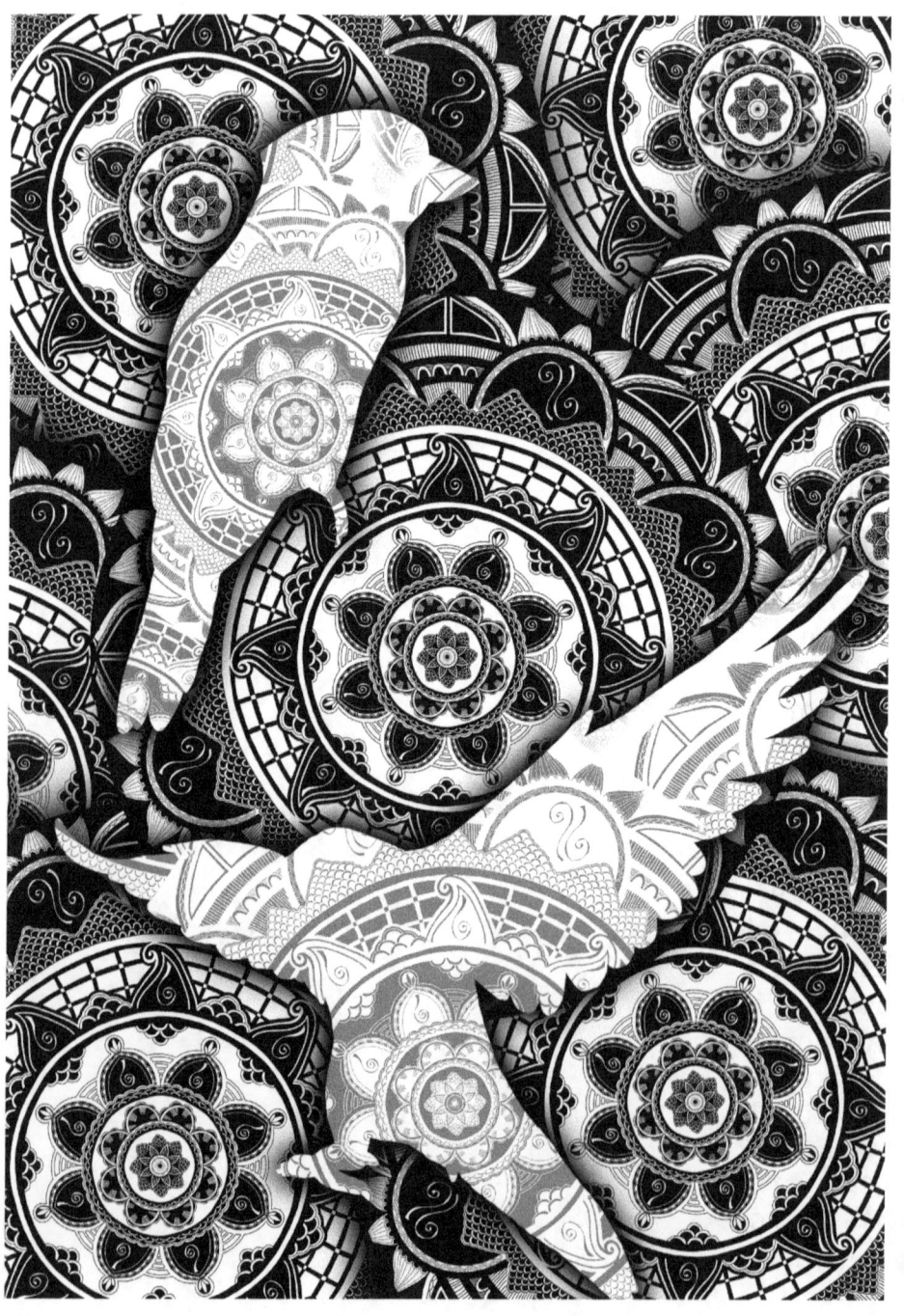

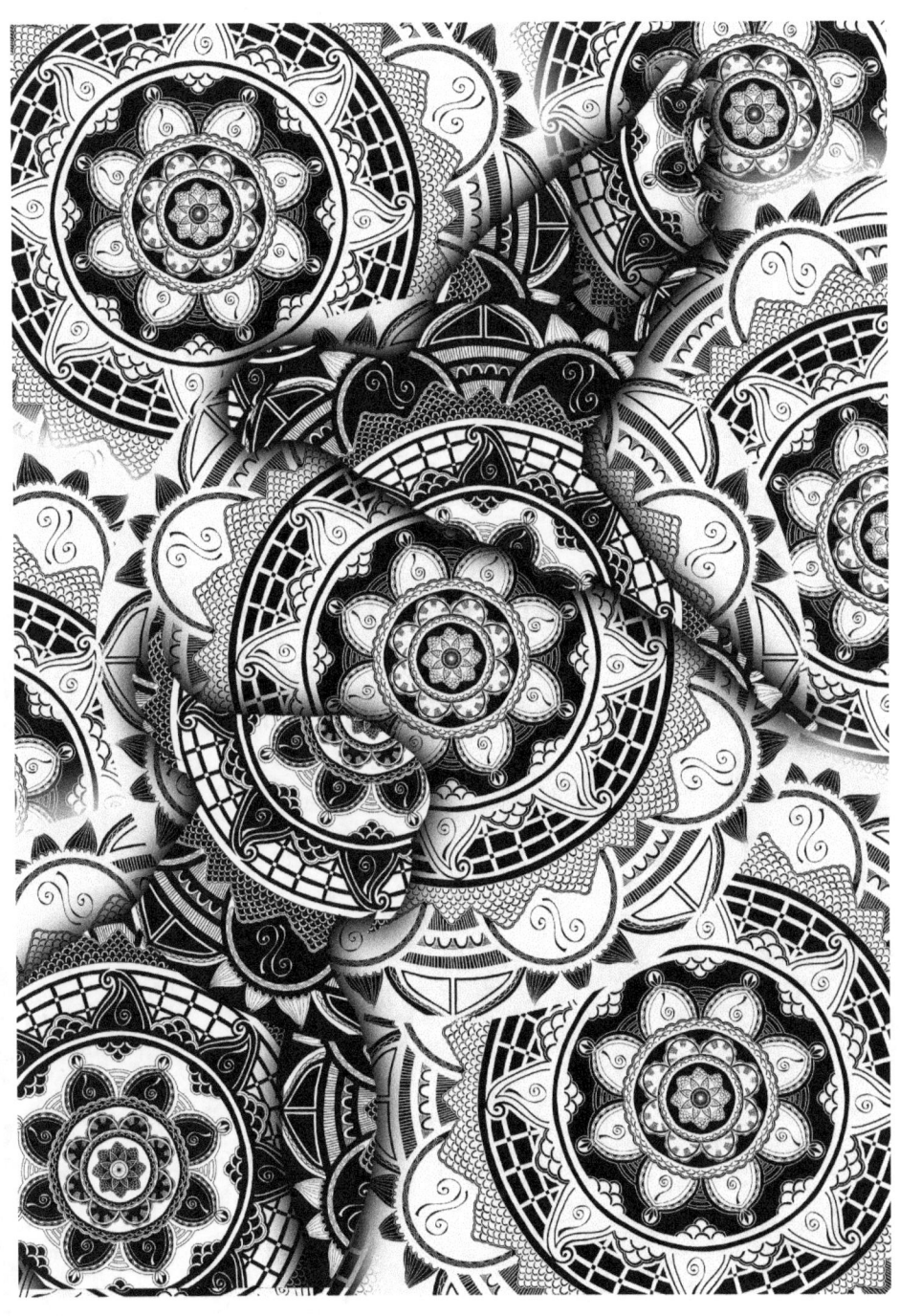

- 1 -

Mist of dawning sun —
Kookaburra awakens
Laughing joyfully

— 2 —

Cockatoo soaring
against rain clouds blushing
grey —
Monochrome palette

- 3 -

Red feathers flitting
through dense verdant
foliage —
Game of peek-a-boo

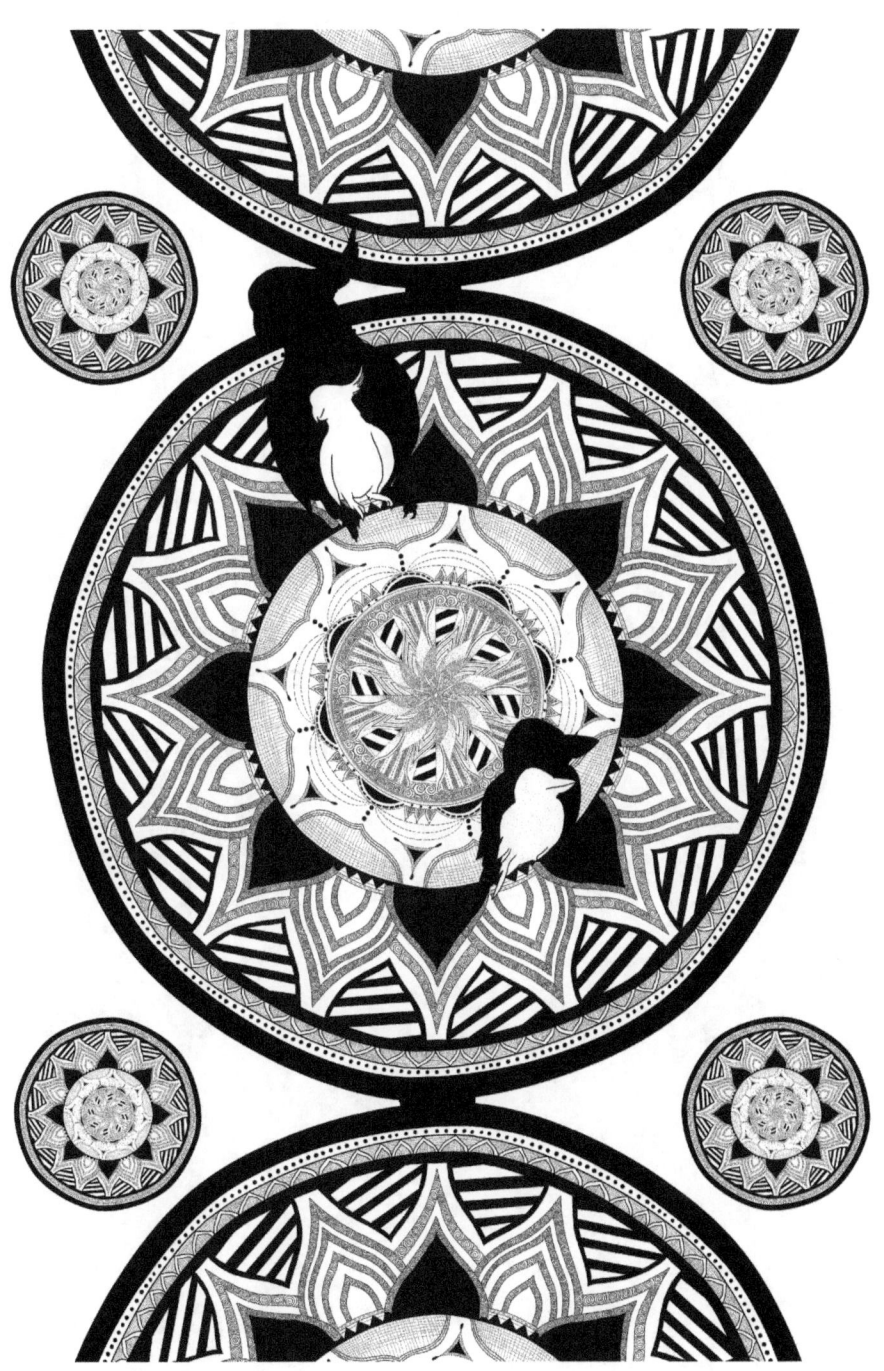

- 4 -

Five in the morning,
A cacophony of caws
from trees dotted white

- 5 -

Feathered bodies a
parody of Greek statues —
Dog is walking by

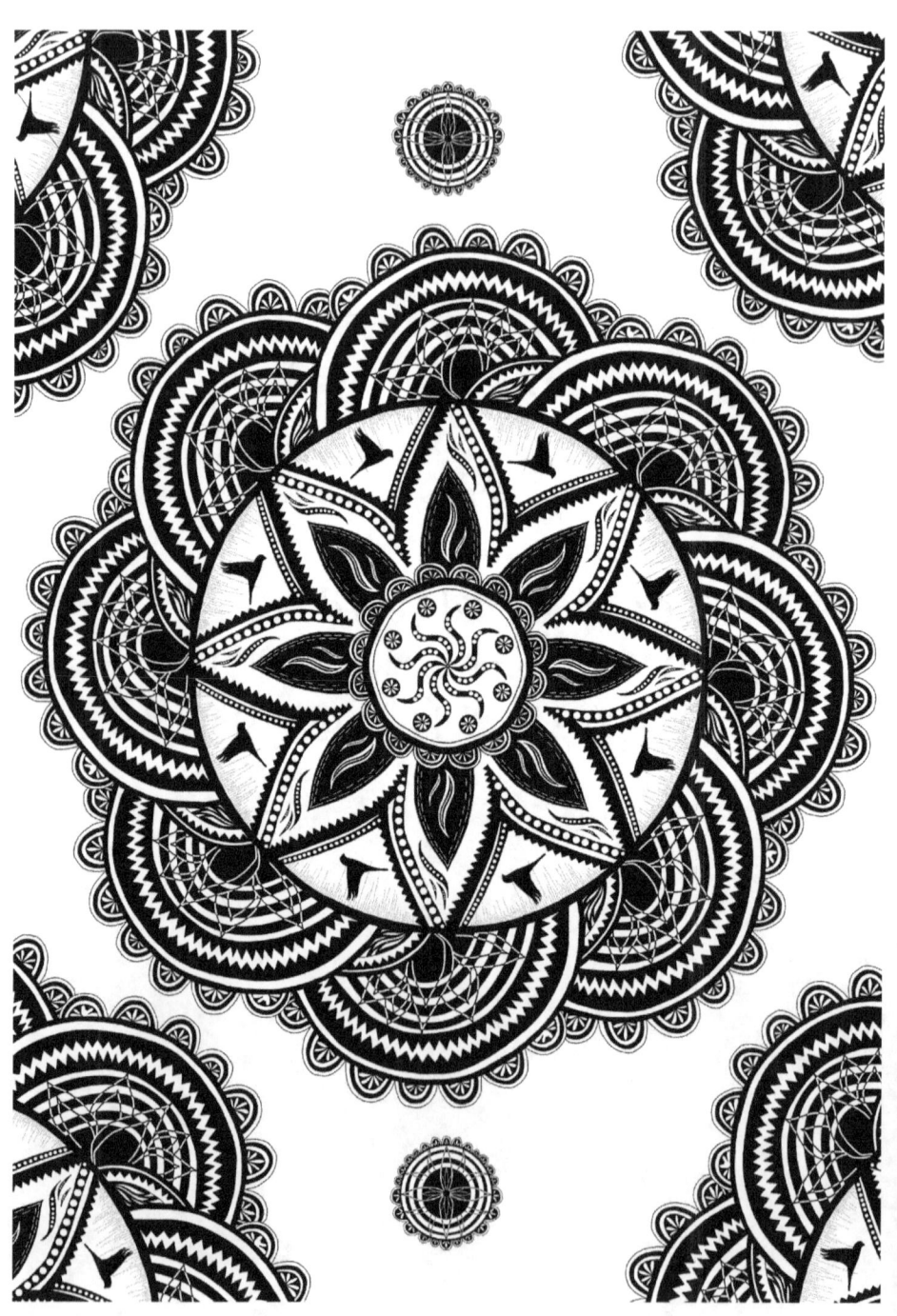

– 6 –

White bodies haloed
against the glare of the sun —
Angels in flight

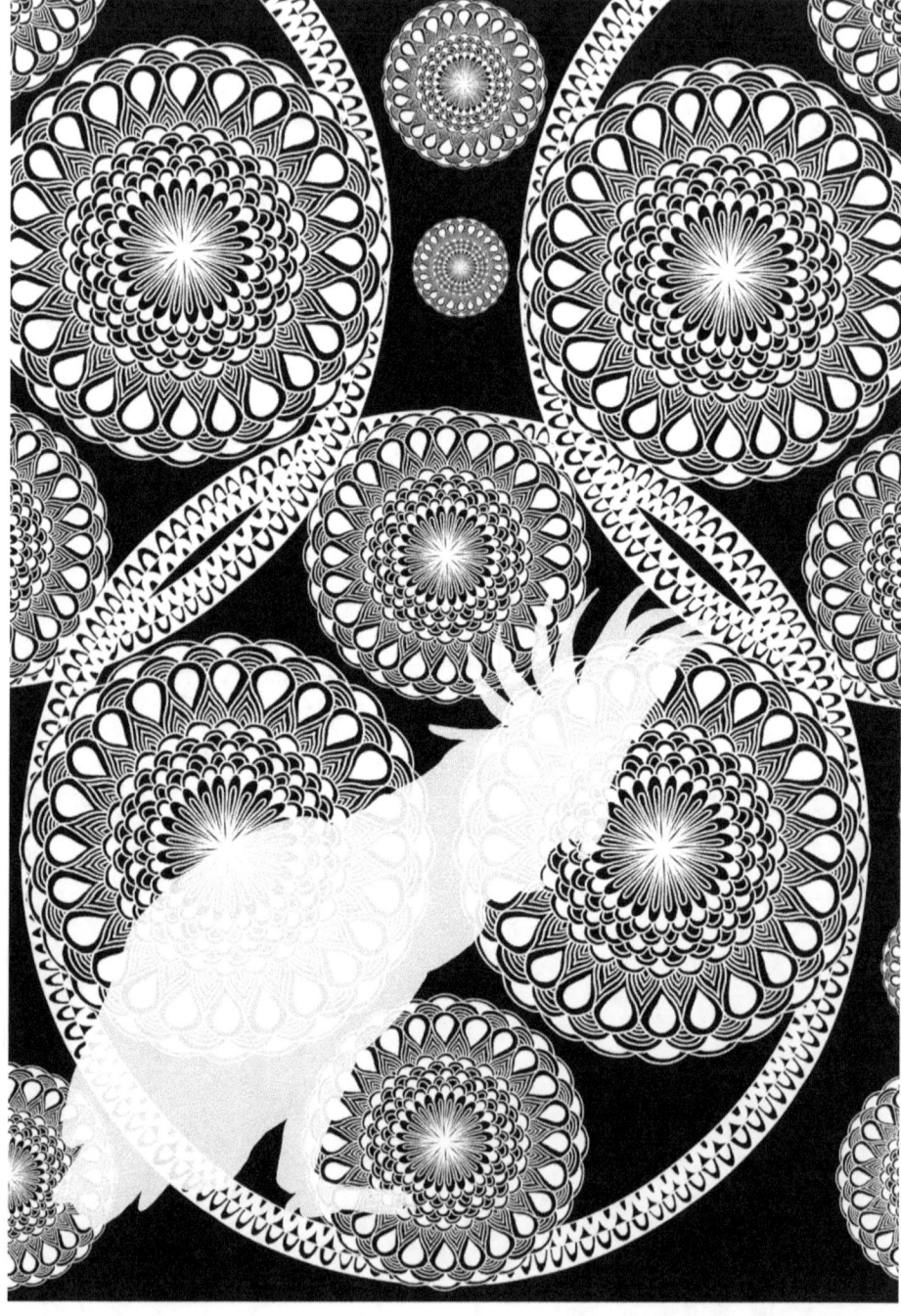

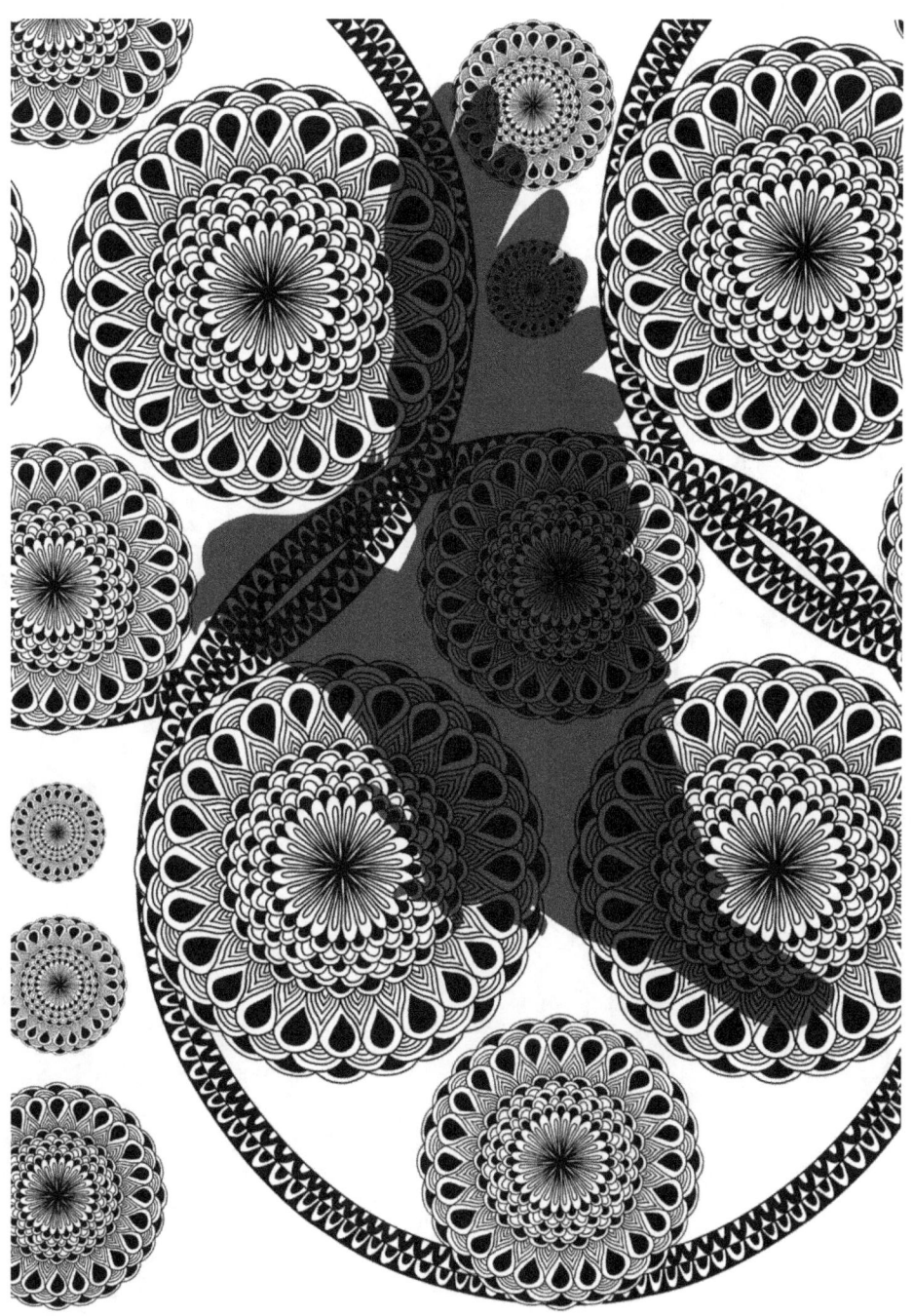

- 7 -

In the blazing heat
A lonely koel cooing
Melodiously

- 8 -

Gum leaves rustle to
an avian symphony —
Teatime by the trees

- 9 -

Unassuming glass —
Battleground for dominance
by angry magpies

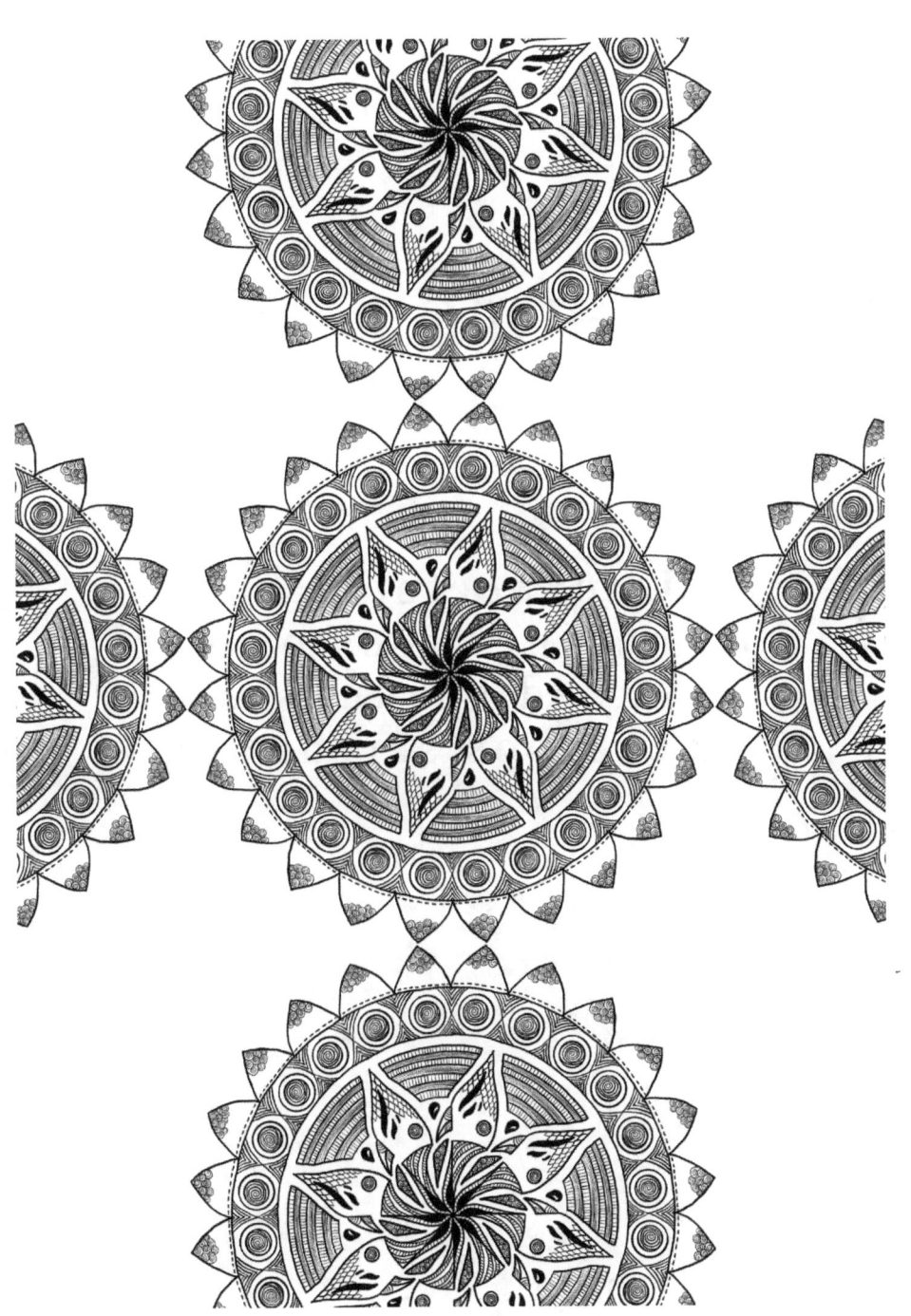

- 10 -

Unexpected rain
Drenching trees on sun
baked grounds—
Cockatoos screaming

- 11 -

Through roaring thunder
A single plaintive quaver —
Little koel sings

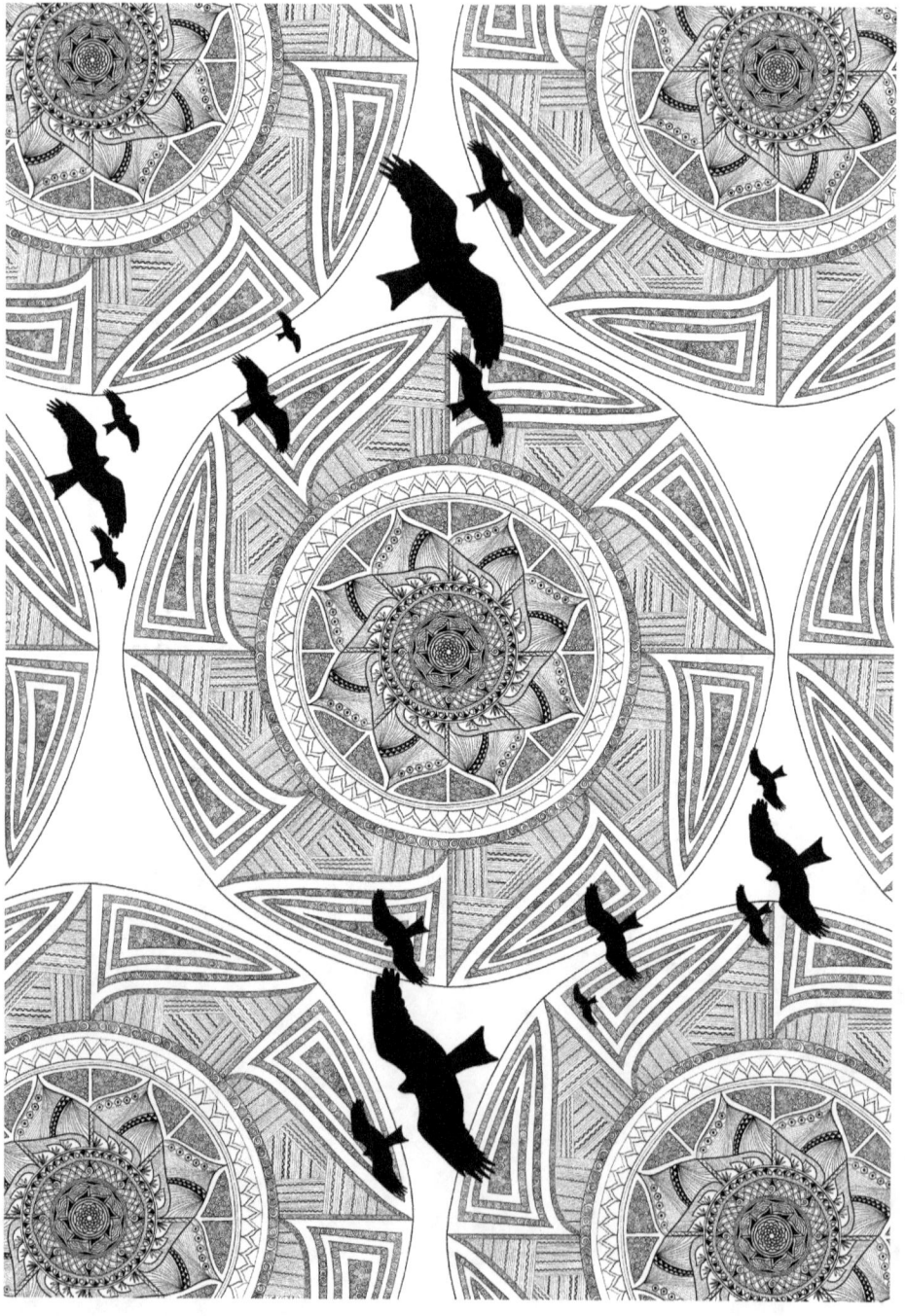

- 12 -

Winter symphony
Rushing to a crescendo
In the crack of dawn

– 13 –

Utility poles —
A brave trapeze artist
swings,
White wings akimbo

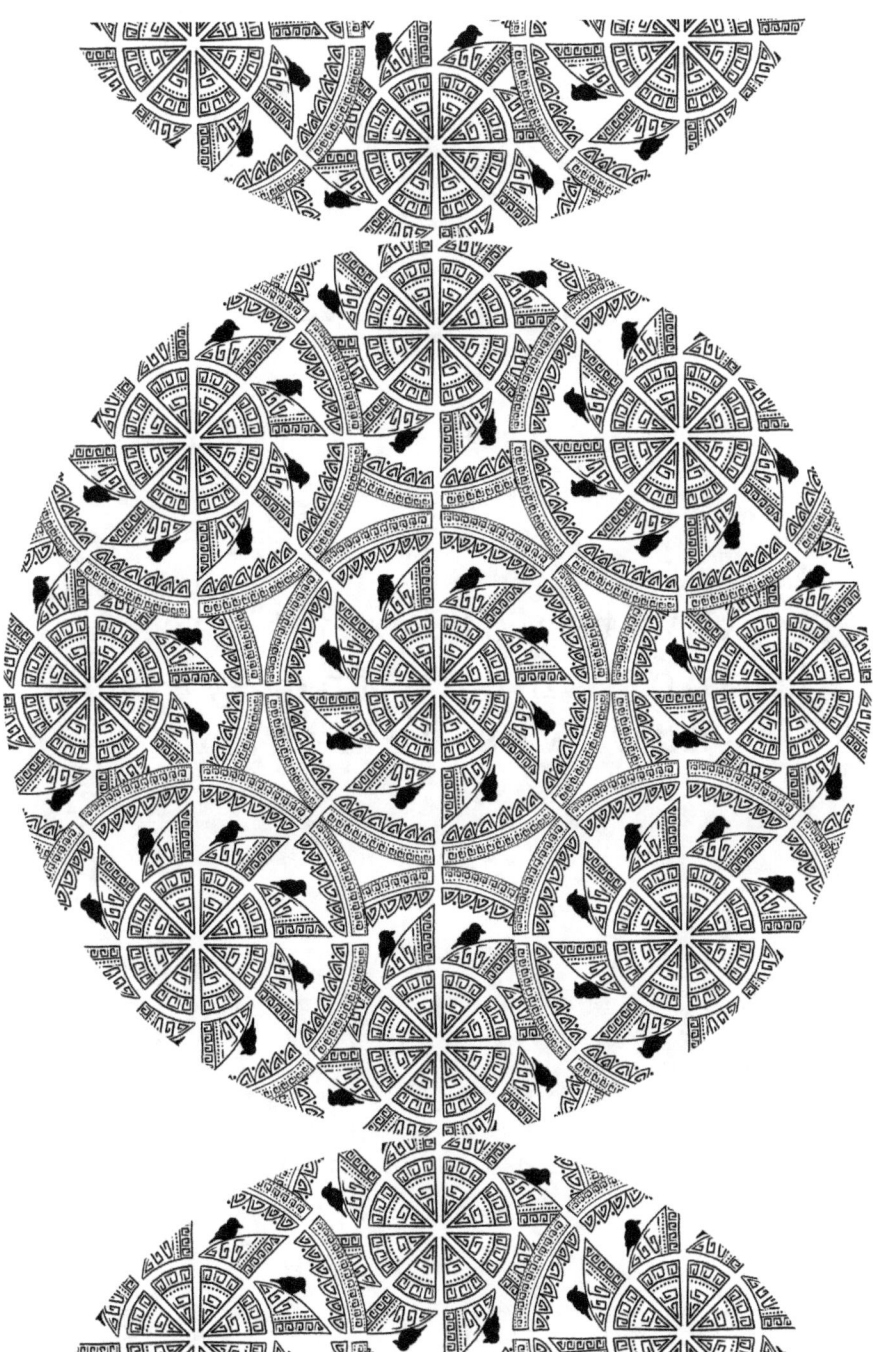

- 14 -

Clatter of roof tiles.
He looks me in the eye and
squawks defiantly.

- 15 -

Amidst sopping leaves
birds unite as one to sing
early winter songs.

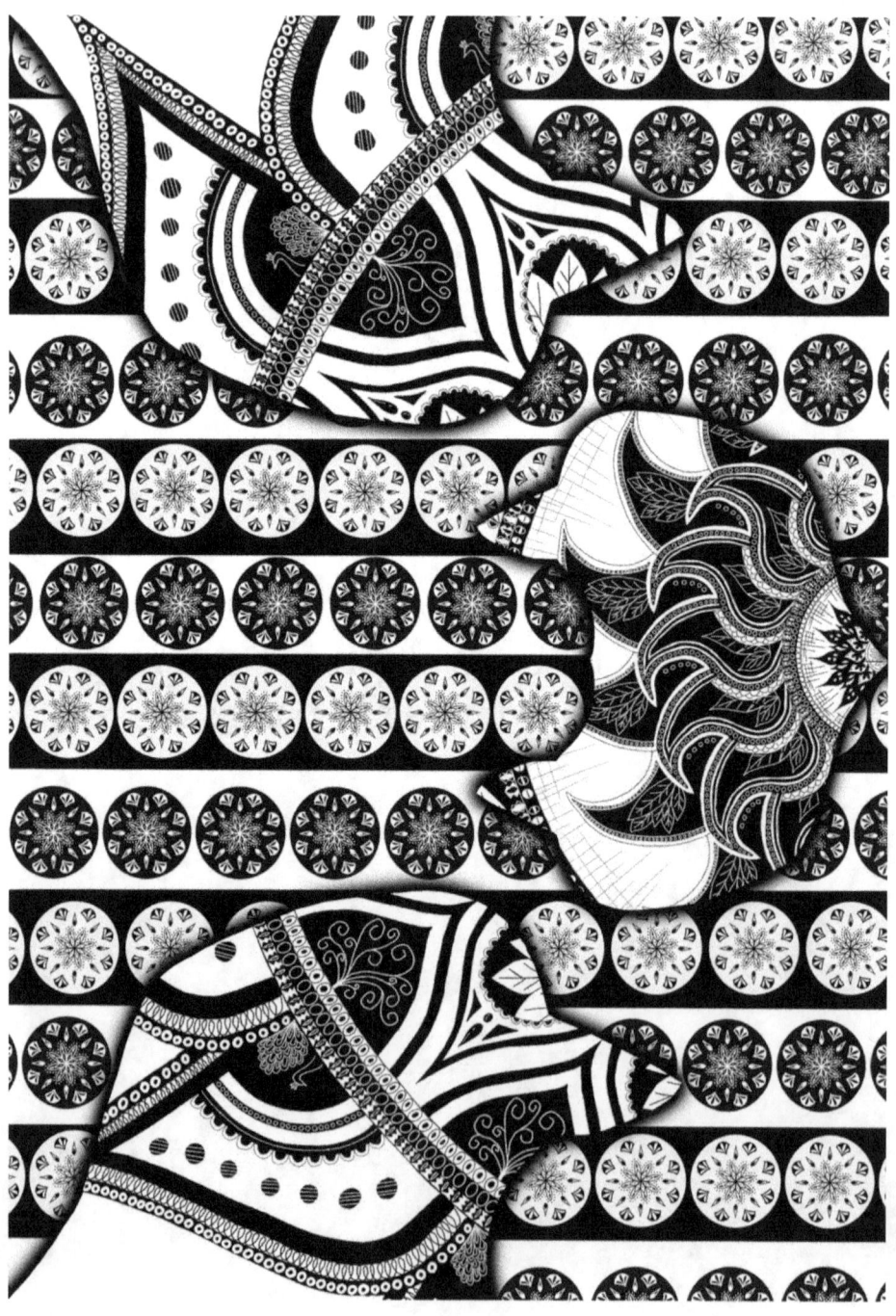

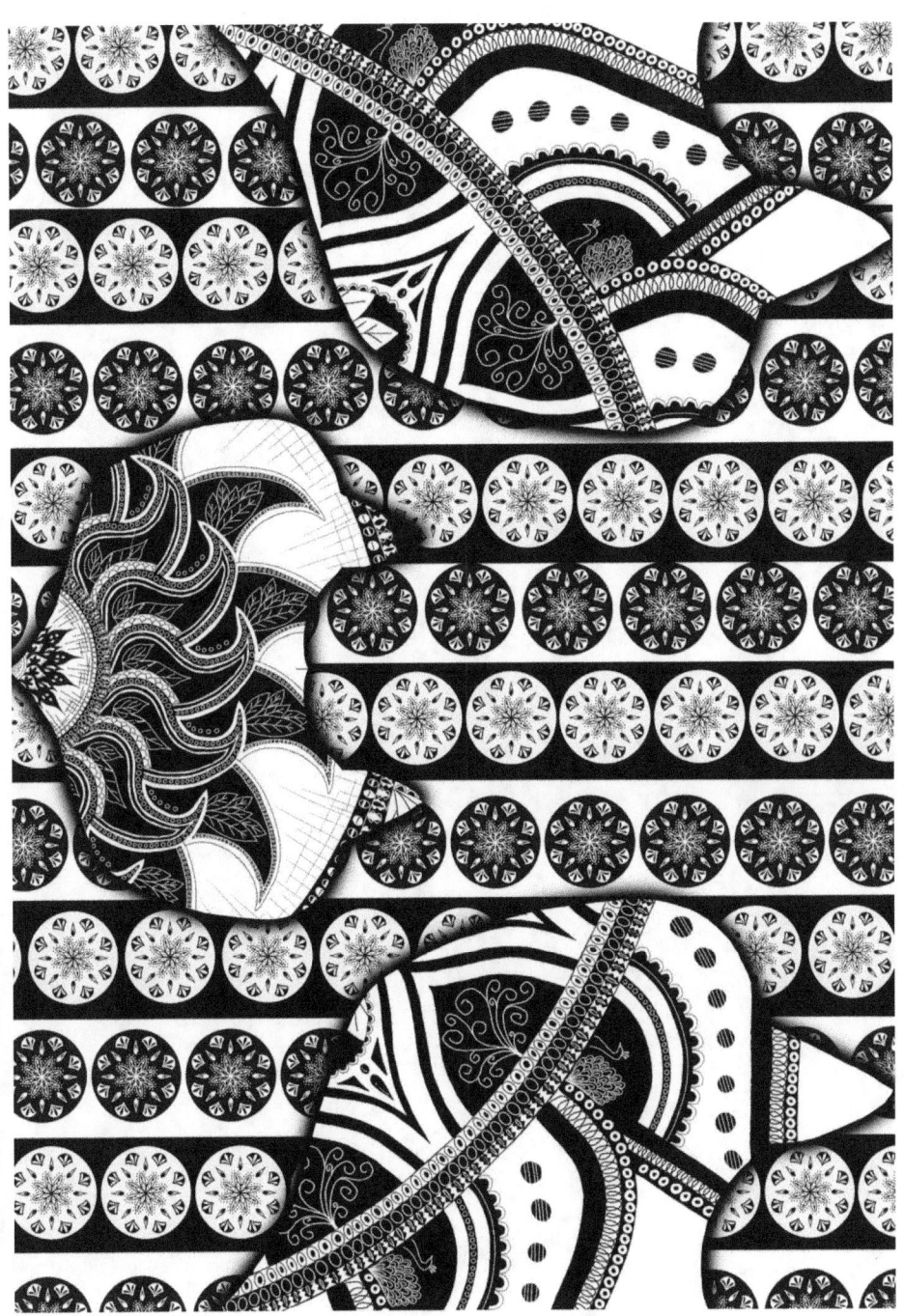

www.ingramcontent.com/pod-product-compliance
Lightning Source LLC
Chambersburg PA
CBHW070959220526
45471CB00007B/3095